27 SPIRITUAL WARFARE POWER PRAYERS & ARMOR OF GOD DEVOTIONAL

FULL-COLOR ILLUSTRATED CHRISTIAN WARRIOR GUIDE: FAITH OVER FEAR, STRENGTH TO STAND FIRM & COURAGE TO CLAIM VICTORY IN LIFE'S BATTLES

GEORGE L. WATERS

STEFANIE L. WATERS

AUTHOR'S NOTE

Dear Reader,

Thank you for choosing our book! We wanted to let you know that there is a companion adult coloring book version of this compilation available as well. Since coloring books cannot be made into ebooks for some major online retailers, we chose to create both a coloring book and a full-color illustrated version of this devotional for you (in both ebook and print formats). Both books contain similar prayers and devotionals, reflection questions and content. Please enjoy the version, or versions, that most appeal to you!

May God bless you,
George & Stefanie

CONTENTS

INTRODUCTION

Put On the Full Armor of God

This illustrated devotional was created to immerse you in the Full Armor of God Warrior Experience, offering powerful tools for spiritual battle with clarity, beauty, and intention. Through a blend of heartfelt prayers, guided reflections, and vivid full-color artwork, this book helps you draw closer to God, your Commander and Protector. Each page is designed to strengthen your connection to Scripture, sharpen your spiritual awareness, and focus your mind on God's Battle Plan.

The book of Ephesians reminds us that the Christian walk is not casual or effortless; it is a daily battle against fear, doubt, temptation, and discouragement. Yet God has not left us unarmed. He equips us with truth, righteousness, faith, salvation, His Word, and His peace; a complete arsenal for every believer who chooses to stand firm.

This devotional invites you to pause, reflect, and intentionally "suit up" with each piece of armor. Walk through Scriptures that call you to courage. Sit with prayers that fortify your spirit. Let the full-color imagery help you visualize the promises of God alive and active in your life. May each page remind you that your strength comes not from your own power, but from the Lord who leads you into victory.

Put on the Full Armor of God and step boldly into the battle.

Deuteronomy 31:8 ~ *"The Lord himself goes before you and will be with you; he will never leave you or forsake you. Do not be afraid; do not be discouraged."*

SPIRITUAL WARFARE PRAYERS & THE CALL TO ARMOR UP

✦ GOD'S BATTLE PLAN ✦

Put on the full armor of God, and call on Him for strength as you step into the battles before you. Every warrior of Christ encounters trials that stretch courage, faith, and conviction. These are not conflicts fought in the natural realm, but spiritual battles — moments when the enemy whispers distortion, when fear attempts to steal your peace, and when temptation tests the foundations of your walk with the Lord. But God has not left His children unguarded. He equips us with divine armor crafted from truth, righteousness, faith, salvation, and His living Word.

When the weight of the world presses against you, remember: your power does not originate from your own resolve. It flows from your Father above.

- The **Belt of Truth** keeps you anchored to what is eternal.
- The **Breastplate of Righteousness** shields your heart from the enemy's accusations.
- The **Sandals of Peace** provide stability as well as readiness for battle.
- The **Shield of Faith** extinguishes every flaming arrow of fear and doubt.
- The **Helmet of Salvation** protects your mind with the certainty of who you are in Christ.
- And the **Sword of the Spirit**, God's unfailing Word, gives you the authority to push back darkness and stand your ground.

As you move through these devotionals, prayers, and visuals, imagine yourself preparing for spiritual battle: tightening the belt, lifting the shield, securing the helmet, gripping the sword. Feel the strength of His presence settle over you like armor. Let each page become a declaration that you are equipped, empowered, and covered.

Even in moments of exhaustion, hold this truth close: **the battle is the Lord's**. You do not fight alone. His strength fills the gaps where yours falters, and His victory has already been declared. Stand firm, Warrior of God. The One who called you is faithful, and He will not fail you.

✦ PRAYER OF PREPARATION FOR BATTLE ✦

Mighty God and Commander of Heaven's Armies,

Prepare me for the battles I will face today. Fasten Your truth around me so deception finds no place to land. Cover my heart with righteousness, that I may stand with integrity, clarity, and holy confidence. Strengthen my faith until it becomes a shield that extinguishes every lie, dart, and scheme of the enemy. Guard my thoughts with the helmet of salvation, reminding me that I am Yours: chosen, redeemed, protected. Place Your Word in my hand like a sharp sword, and ignite my spirit with Your power and presence.

When fear whispers, let Your peace rise like a fortress.

When darkness presses in, let Your strength drive it back.

Teach me to battle not through human effort, but through complete reliance on You, the Lord of Hosts who goes before me, stands beside me, and secures every victory on my behalf.

In the mighty name of Jesus, Amen.

POWER PRINCIPLE

Today, I take my place as a warrior clothed in Your armor and empowered, equipped, and appointed for triumph.

Dedicated to:
ALRUN SOUTHWICK MILLIGAN

Our mother, whose faith never falters and
whose love for Christ burns
brighter through every storm.

Steadfast in spirit, unyielding in faith, and
unashamed of the Gospel, your devotion to
Christ and His Word is a living testament to the
power of unwavering belief and the strength
of a warrior's heart.

With Love,
Larry & Stefanie

1 Corinthians 16:13
"Be on your guard;
stand firm in the faith;
be courageous; be strong."

PART ONE
THIS IS YOUR CALL
TO ARMOR UP (THE
FOUNDATION)

THE CALL TO ARMOR UP

We first receive the call to "armor up" in the book of Ephesians. Before a single blow is struck, God issues a clear directive: **stand**; not trembling, not retreating, but anchored in unwavering faith. The battle Paul describes is not poetic imagery; it is the ongoing war fought in our thoughts, our families, our choices, and our spiritual life. And in this conflict, God has never expected His people to fight while exposed. He clothes His warriors in armor forged by His own power, armor no darkness can break, no enemy can overcome: the Full Armor of God.

Ephesians 6:10–12 ~ *"Finally, be strong in the Lord and in His mighty power. Put on the full armor of God, so that you can take your stand against the devil's schemes. For our struggle is not against flesh and blood, but against the rulers, against the authorities, against the powers of this dark world and against the spiritual forces of evil in the heavenly realms."*

TRUE STRENGTH DOESN'T RISE from our own abilities, achievements, or willpower; it comes directly from God. Just as salvation is a gift we cannot earn, His strength is something He freely pours into us. Scripture reminds us that human armor has no power in the kind of battles we face. The enemy's attacks are not physical; they're subtle, invisible, and spiritual. Because we wrestle with forces we cannot see, earthly defenses are useless. Only God's supernatural armor can withstand a supernatural enemy.

Ephesians 6:13 ~ *"Therefore take up the whole armor of God, that you*

may be able to withstand in the evil day, and having done all, to stand firm."

THE FULL ARMOR of God empowers His children to stand firm in the face of spiritual darkness without retreating, without being intimidated, and without falling into defeat. One translation makes the reality unmistakable: *"so when the day of evil comes ..."* Not **if**, but **when**. Scripture prepares us for the certainty that every believer will face the enemy's attacks. The only question is whether we will be equipped. And the only way to be equipped is to put on **all** of God's armor.

Emphasis is placed on the *whole* armor because anything less leaves openings the enemy can exploit. God provides a complete, impenetrable defense: His truth, His righteousness, His peace, His faith, His salvation, and His Word, so that we can stand against every strategy of the Devil.

In Ephesians 6:10–13, two commands rise to the forefront:

- **Be strong.**
- **And know exactly where to go for that strength.**

Strength is obtained, not from ourselves, not from the world, but from the Lord who empowers us for the battle.

🗡 ***Ephesians 6:14–17*** *~ "Stand therefore, having fastened on the belt of truth, and having put on the breastplate of righteousness, and, as shoes for your feet, having put on the readiness given by the gospel of peace. In all circumstances take up the shield of faith, with which you can extinguish all the flaming darts of the evil one; and take the helmet of salvation, and the sword of the Spirit, which is the word of God."*

EACH PIECE of God's armor is described with intention. Nothing is accidental, and nothing is optional.

THE BELT OF TRUTH

The Belt of Truth is the anchor of the entire armor. It secures everything in place and keeps the soldier free from distraction or entanglement. Without truth, every other piece loses stability. A soldier trying to fight without a belt would stumble long before the enemy ever touched him.

THE BREASTPLATE OF RIGHTEOUSNESS

The Breastplate of Righteousness guards the most vulnerable areas: the heart, the lungs, the core of life itself. It protects from arrows you never saw coming and glancing blows that could take you down in close combat. Righteousness, given by God, shields you from attacks both distant and sudden.

THE SANDALS OF PEACE

The Sandals of Peace give the believer sure footing. Roman soldiers wore **caligae**: heavy-duty leather sandals with iron studs driven into the soles. These were the world's first "cleats," allowing soldiers to stand firm on slippery or uneven terrain without being pushed back or faltering. They represent readiness rooted in the gospel: stability, traction, and the ability to move with purpose. No soldier marches into battle in flimsy shoes. The right footing prevents slips, falls, and hesitation, enabling you to stand firm when the ground shakes.

THE SHIELD OF FAITH

The Shield of Faith is essential from every angle. It blocks the immediate strikes and intercepts the long-distance attacks: the fiery darts aimed at your mind, your confidence, your hope. Because the enemy fires without warning and from every direction, the shield is a constant, indispensable defense.

THE HELMET OF SALVATION

The Helmet of Salvation protects the mind: the place where fear, doubt, and confusion try to take root. A single blow here can end the fight. This helmet reminds you who you belong to and shields your thoughts from lies that attempt to destabilize your faith.

THE SWORD OF THE SPIRIT

The Sword of the Spirit (the Word of God) is unique among the armor because it is both defensive and offensive. It allows you to deflect spiritual attacks and also strike back with truth that sends the enemy retreating into the darkness. It is power in motion, authority in your hand, and victory spoken aloud.

SPIRITUAL WARFARE PRAYERS
NOTES

SPIRITUAL WARFARE PRAYER - THE POWER OF PRAYER

Almighty Father, Lord who hears from Heaven,

Today, I come before You not with eloquence, but with the raw cry of a warrior's spirit. I know prayer is not quiet or passive. It is battle. When I lift my voice, strongholds shake, darkness recoils, and Heaven moves at Your command. Train me to pray with relentless courage. Let every request I make pierce the enemy's territory like arrows of holy light. When exhaustion pulls at me, renew my strength. When my voice grows faint, let the Holy Spirit speak through me with power. Shape me into a soldier who bows before You first, so I can stand firm against every attack that rises.

Let my prayers become weapons of victory, my praise become warfare, and my faith burn like fire.

Amen.

POWER PRINCIPLE

I declare that every triumph begins here: on my knees before You.

SPIRITUAL WARFARE PRAYER - VICTORY THROUGH CHRIST

Triumphant Savior, King of Glory,

The battle may roar around me, but the final outcome has never been in question. The victory is already Yours. Remind me that I am seated with You in heavenly places, lifted far above the reach of fear, defeat, or intimidation. Let Your triumph become the anthem of my heart, Your strength the anchor of my confidence, and Your Spirit the force that carries me forward. When the enemy taunts, I will worship. When the war intensifies, I will rest in the power of Your finished work. You have already overcome death, darkness, and every force that rises against Your people.

Amen.

POWER PRINCIPLE

I declare that same victory over my life today.

SPIRITUAL WARFARE PRAYER - STRENGTH FOR THE BATTLE

Mighty Lord, my Defender and Commander of Heaven's Armies,

Today, I rise to meet the unseen battles ahead. Though the enemy whispers distortion and doubt, I plant my feet firmly in Your truth. I refuse to fight in fear, in panic, or in human strength. Instead, I take my place in the armor You've provided, remaining steady, alert, and ready for whatever comes.

Strengthen my hands for warfare and fortify my heart with endurance. Let Your truth direct my steps, Your Spirit fuel my resolve, and Your Word become the weapon that cuts through every lie. When doubt tries to take root, uproot it with faith. When the world presses hard against me, remind me that You go before me as my defender and my victory. I belong to You; covered in light, set apart for battle, and walking in triumph secured at the cross.

In the name of Jesus Christ, my Warrior-King, Amen.

POWER PRINCIPLE

I will not retreat. I will not surrender.

SPIRITUAL WARFARE PRAYER - THE HELMET OF SALVATION

Savior and Redeemer, Captain of My Soul

Lord, place the Helmet of Salvation securely over my mind. Shield my thoughts from confusion, deception, and fear. Let the confidence of my salvation rest on me like a crown no enemy can challenge or remove. When the real battle begins in my thoughts, speak Your peace into the deepest places of my spirit. Silence every whisper of condemnation and remind me continually that I belong to You.

Renew my mind day by day.

Align my thoughts with Your truth: that I am redeemed, chosen, and marked for victory.

Guard me from distraction, doubt, and mental warfare.

Teach me to think as a child of light: disciplined, clear-minded, and courageous.

*Let every thought be brought captive to **Jesus Christ**, anchored in grace and held firm by Your love.*

Amen.

POWER PRINCIPLE

Today I wear salvation as my armor, my proof of triumph, my seal of identity, and my reminder that the victory has already been won.

DEVOTIONAL 1: THE CALL TO ARMOR UP

Every believer encounters spiritual battles: the quiet moments of temptation, the unexpected waves of doubt, and the unseen resistance that pushes against your walk with God. Paul reminds us in Ephesians 6 that our struggle is not against flesh and blood, but against the spiritual forces of darkness. This is why the full armor of God is not optional; it is essential.

We cannot stand firm through human strength alone. The belt of truth keeps us grounded. The breastplate of righteousness shields our hearts. The shield of faith extinguishes every fiery attack. The helmet of salvation guards our thoughts, and the sword of the Spirit (the living Word of God) equips us to advance with confidence.

As you move through these pages, let the full-color imagery help you envision each piece of God's armor being placed upon you. Pause, breathe, and ask the Lord to empower you with His strength. Remember, victory doesn't begin with force; it starts with surrender to the One who fights on your behalf.

🙏 *Prayer: "Lord, clothe me today with Your armor. Strengthen me to stand firm, not in my power, but in Yours."*

REFLECTION QUESTIONS

The Call to Armor Up ✦

1. **Which part of God's armor is most essential for you in this season?**
   - Is it truth to steady your mind, righteousness to guard your heart, faith to shield you, salvation to anchor your identity, peace to steady your steps, or the Word to strengthen your spirit?
2. **What does it look like for you to "stand firm" right now?**
   - How is God calling on you to hold your ground, stay rooted, or remain unshaken in the middle of your current battles?

PART TWO
YES, GOD IS
OUR FORTRESS
(PROTECTION)

GOD IS YOUR PROTECTION

When the battle intensifies and fear tries to press in, we turn to the One who stands as our true refuge, a sanctuary not crafted by human hands, but anchored in the unshakable strength of God Himself. He is our firm foundation, our shield, our fortress in every storm. In His presence, no weapon can succeed, and no shadow can overcome His light. Beneath His covering, we find calm; within His fortress, we are secure. The Lord is not only the One who guards us, He is the very safeguard that surrounds us.

> **Psalm 18:2** ~ *"The Lord is my rock and my fortress and my deliverer, my God, my rock, in whom I take refuge, my shield, and the horn of my salvation, my stronghold."*

A MILLENNIUM before Paul penned the instructive and battle-ready passage that we now recognize as Ephesians 6, we see the Psalmist was already revealing the power and urgency of a vital piece of God's Armor ... the Shield of Faith. Although King David may not have used Paul's exact wording, he clearly described the same truth: he placed his confidence in the protective strength of the Lord. In doing so, David was pointing to the very shield Paul would later urge the believers in Ephesus to lift up as their defense. Both men, separated by centuries, declared the same message: that God Himself is the shield that guards His people.

In Psalm 18:2, King David proclaims with absolute confidence that his entire trust in a protector and rescuer lies in the Lord God. He goes on to describe God's unwavering strength through a series of timeless metaphors; images so powerful they've echoed through Christian teaching, worship songs, and church traditions across generations.

Think about how many of these metaphors you have personally used or heard used throughout your life to describe God's protective nature. God is our rock, our deliverer, our fortress, our refuge, shield, and stronghold. Each metaphor paints a different picture of how God surrounds, defends, and upholds His people in moments of need. Together, they remind us that His protection is complete, dependable, and fiercely personal.

 Psalm 91:1–2 ~ *"Whoever dwells in the shelter of the Most High will rest in the shadow of the Almighty. I will say of the Lord, 'He is my refuge and my fortress, my God, in whom I trust.'"*

THESE VERSES REVEAL A DEEPLY personal relationship with God, one marked by continual closeness and steady communion. To "dwell" in His shelter speaks of more than momentary protection; it describes an ongoing intimacy with the Almighty. Another translation calls it "the secret place of the Most High," a phrase that captures the idea of living in God's presence day by day. This isn't a refuge we run to only when life turns chaotic; it's a place where the believer chooses to remain, whether the path is stormy or serene. It highlights a consistent ongoing relationship with God, where the Christian remains in constant communion with the Almighty, seeking closeness to Him not just in times of trouble, but also when the waters are smooth.

In this sacred place of closeness, God's people experience a depth of protection that empowers them to boldly call Him their personal fortress and refuge. It reflects a relationship built on trust, not distance, and the assurance that we are held by a God who knows us intimately. The imagery of His "shadow" evokes the tenderness of a mother bird covering her young, a picture of constant nearness and protective care. It reminds believers that God's presence is steady, His promise to guard us, spiritually and physically, is unbroken.

The Psalmist ends verse two with the confidence of someone who has lived under God's covering and knows firsthand the strength that comes from placing complete trust in Him.

 Psalm 91:4 ~ *"He will cover you with his pinions, and under his wings you will find refuge; his faithfulness is a shield and buckler."*

PSALM 91:4 deepens this imagery by portraying God as a protective mother bird who gathers her young beneath her wings. It's a picture of refuge that is both strong and tender. His wings symbolize a covering that shields us in moments of danger, yet also surrounds us with warmth and reassurance. Like a mother sheltering her chicks, God offers a place where we are not only defended from harm but soothed by His calming presence. His protection isn't mechanical or obligatory; it flows from His personal love, His compassion, and His desire to hold His children close.

Isaiah 54:17 ~ "No weapon that is fashioned against you shall succeed, and you shall refute every tongue that rises against you in judgment. This is the heritage of the servants of the Lord and their vindication from me, declares the Lord."

IN ISAIAH 54:17, believers are given a profound promise of God's supernatural protection; a reassurance that reaches even further than the refuge described in the Psalms. Here, God declares that any weapon, whether physical or spiritual, crafted against His people, will ultimately fail. It is not merely that we are defended; it is that the schemes of our enemies are destined to collapse under the authority of the Almighty.

This promise is more than encouragement; it is an inheritance. As God's children and co-heirs with Christ, we receive this protection not because we have earned it, but because He freely gives it. Just as salvation is a gift of grace, so is the covering He places over our lives.

The word "divine" carries weight here. It signifies complete, flawless authority. God is reminding us that He reigns over every circumstance, every threat, every adversary. Our safety is secure because His power is unmatched, and His control is absolute.

This passage concludes with God's firm stance against any voice that would accuse or condemn His people. He Himself promises vindication. Once again, He extends what we could never earn (righteousness, protection, and victory) and provides us these gifts given out of His boundless love.

SPIRITUAL WARFARE PRAYER - FAITH THAT MOVES MOUNTAINS

God of the Impossible, Mover of Mountains,

You declared that even the smallest seed of faith can move what seems unmovable. When doubt tries to rise, strengthen my belief. Teach me to speak with confidence, not because of my own ability, but because of Your unmatched authority. Let every mountain of fear, sickness, discouragement, or despair crumble at the sound of Your command. Breathe bold, unwavering faith into my spirit, Lord. Fill me with courage that refuses to back down.

Amen.

POWER PRINCIPLE

Today I proclaim that nothing is impossible for the one who believes in You.

SPIRITUAL WARFARE PRAYER – THE LORD IS MY REFUGE

Mighty Fortress, My Shelter and Shield,

When the enemy presses in, I run straight into Your presence. You are my refuge, my fortified tower, the place where darkness loses its power. Under the covering of Your wings, no threat can touch me, and no shadow can overtake me. When the world feels uncertain or unsafe, remind me that Your protection is my shield and my victory. Teach me to remain in Your shadow, to live there, not merely visit, when trouble comes. You are my shelter, my defender, and the One who surrounds me with unshakable strength.

Amen.

POWER PRINCIPLE

I accept Your divine protection, and I take refuge in Your name. There I stand, unbreakable.

SPIRITUAL WARFARE PRAYER - THE BREASTPLATE OF RIGHTEOUSNESS

Righteous Father, My Shield and Defender,

*Lord, guard my heart today with the covering of Your righteousness. I set aside pride, shame, guilt, and every false defense, for none of these can protect me. Only the righteousness You place upon me can silence the enemy's accusations. Wrap my heart in purity, strength, and grace that flow from You alone. When condemnation tries to speak, remind me that I stand justified by the blood of **Jesus Christ**. When my own shortcomings attempt to strike, tighten Your armor around me until I feel fully secured in Your mercy.*

Align my heartbeat with Yours: steady, forgiven, fearless.

Let my life reflect Your holiness in every step and every choice.

May righteousness shine from me like light breaking through armor, pushing back the darkness without fear or shame.

Clothe me in Your righteousness, Lord, so no weapon can find its mark.

Amen.

POWER PRINCIPLE

I am Yours, and in Your strength, I walk in victory.

SPIRITUAL WARFARE PRAYER – THE SANDALS OF PEACE

Prince of Peace, My Steadfast Guide,

Lord, fasten my feet with the sandals of Your peace. As I move through moments of chaos, conflict, or uncertainty, let me walk with steady confidence, knowing You've already gone ahead of me. When the ground feels unstable, strengthen my footing. When others stir up tension, teach me to carry Your peace into every space I enter. May every step I take leave behind a trace of Your presence.

I refuse to walk in fear. I choose to walk in faith.

Root me in Your Word until peace becomes the posture of my life, stronger than confusion, louder than fear, and deeper than pain. Guide my path with holy calmness and divine assurance, shaping my steps with wisdom and courage.

Amen.

POWER PRINCIPLE

I do not walk by my own power, but in the authority of Jesus Christ, the One who stilled the storm.

DEVOTIONAL 2: GOD IS OUR FORTRESS

✦ Safe in His Shadow✦

The Psalmist proclaims that God is our rock, our fortress, and our deliverer; the One we can run to when the winds rise, when enemies press in, or when fear whispers in the shadows. His refuge cannot be shaken. Under His wings, we are calmed. Behind His shield, we are protected.

Far too often, we try to anchor ourselves in fragile worldly things like people, plans, routines, or possessions, forgetting that only God is a fortress capable of holding the full weight of our lives. Scripture reminds us that no weapon formed against His children will succeed, because His presence surrounds us like fortified walls.

As you move through these pages and reflect on the images before you, imagine stepping into that divine stronghold and being completely covered, fully seen, utterly safe. Breathe deeply and settle into this truth: the Almighty Himself is your refuge, and *He will not fail you.*

🙏 *Prayer: "Father, thank you that You are my shield and my fortress. Hide me under Your wings and let me rest in the safety of Your presence."*

REFLECTION QUESTIONS

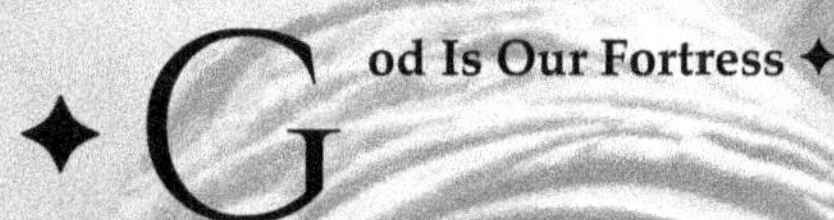

✦ **G**od Is Our Fortress ✦

REFLECT ON THESE QUESTIONS:

1. **When life presses hard against you, where do you instinctively seek comfort or protection first?**
   - What would it look like to redirect your steps and take refuge in God as your true fortress?
2. **What fear, worry, or heavy burden can you release into God's keeping today?**
   - What can you place beneath His covering and allow Him to carry for you?

PART THREE
HAVE COURAGE
IN THE BATTLE
(STRENGTH)

COURAGE IN THE BATTLE

Every warrior of God encounters moments when fear speaks louder than confidence, yet Scripture calls us to stand our ground. Courage isn't the absence of fear; it's having faith and choosing to move forward anyway. The same God who commanded Joshua to step into unknown waters, the same God who strengthened David on the battlefield, is the God who stands beside you right now. When the night feels heavy and the enemy seems close, hold tight to this unbreakable truth: the Lord fights for you, shields you, and never abandons His own. Take heart, mighty warrior, as your strength flows from the One who has *never lost a battle.*

Deuteronomy 31:6 ~ *"Be strong and courageous. Do not fear or be in dread of them, for it is the Lord your God who goes with you. He will not leave you or forsake you."*

IN THIS PASSAGE, God isn't simply offering comfort. He's issuing a clear command. Earlier Scriptures remind us of everything He provides for His people, but here the focus shifts. God tells us exactly what is required of us if we want to walk fully in His promises. And even as He commands us, He also makes it unmistakably clear that the ability to obey comes from relying completely on Him.

Courage is not something we create or muster through willpower. It doesn't originate in our personality or our natural strength. Courage is breathed into us by God. True strength rises when we let go of our human limits and tap into the supernatural power of the One who freely shares His strength with His children.

God commands us not to fear, not to be shaken, not to bow to intimidation. He calls us into a confidence that can only exist because His presence outweighs every threat, every enemy, every obstacle that stands against us. Our faith rests on His promise that He will never abandon, desert, or leave us unprotected. That assurance has carried generations before us, and it stands unbroken today. The Holy Spirit surrounds you even now with protection, comfort, and a peace that cannot be shaken.

> *Joshua 1:9* ~ *"Have I not commanded you? Be strong and courageous. Do not be frightened, and do not be dismayed, for the Lord your God is with you wherever you go."*

THIS VERSE DOESN'T JUST REMIND us of God's command to be courageous. It reinforces it with absolute certainty. God isn't hesitating, and He isn't offering a suggestion. He is making His intention unmistakably clear. We are meant to take this command, plant it deep in our hearts, and let it shape the way we walk, think, and respond to life's battles.

Just as He promised in Deuteronomy, God assures us that courage is met with His constant presence. He emphasizes His authority and repeats the instruction so we don't mistake its weight. When God says He will be with us "wherever you go," He is declaring a promise that knows no boundaries. It is not dependent on circumstance, location, or timing. It stands firm; a foundational truth meant to anchor the courage He commands us to carry.

Joshua 1:9 becomes evidence of the deeply personal connection between God's presence and the courage we are called to display. It calls believers to choose faith over fear, to lean on God's strength rather than their own, and to trust that His promises are more reliable than anything we can muster in our own power. The message is clear: our abilities may be limited, but God's faithfulness never is. His presence will always carry us through.

> *2 Thessalonians 3:3* ~ *"But the Lord is faithful. He will strengthen you and protect you from the evil one."*

IN THIS PASSAGE, Paul offers the believer deep reassurance, reminding us of God's unwavering faithfulness and His promise to strengthen and guard us from evil. This verse becomes an anchor in seasons of uncertainty, a steadying truth that fills the cracks where doubt tries to settle. It affirms that God is not distant, distracted, or inconsistent. He is ever-present, ever-protective, and endlessly loving.

Paul underscores that God's character is rock-solid and unchanging. His faithfulness isn't a trait He occasionally displays; it is the core of who He is. He keeps every promise. He never fails His children. And woven into this assurance is the pledge that God Himself will supply the strength we need. As we've seen, true strength and courage don't rise from our own limited humanity; they come from surrendering to God's supernatural power at work within us. Through that surrender, the Lord equips us to endure hardship, resist temptation, and stand firm against every attack the enemy attempts.

SPIRITUAL WARFARE PRAYER - MORE THAN CONQUERORS

Victorious Christ, Lord God All Powerful,

*You have declared that in every circumstance we rise as more than conquerors through the power of Your love. Even when trials press in, and the enemy roars loudly, no force in Heaven, on earth, or in the unseen can pull me away from Your embrace. Let this truth become my battle cry: **the victory has already been secured.** When the fight feels long and relentless, turn my eyes to the cross, the place where the outcome was finalized by **Jesus Christ.** Strengthen me to endure with purpose, to persevere with joy, and to overcome with grace that only You can supply.*

Amen.

POWER PRINCIPLE

Lord, I advance as a conqueror crowned in Your glory: unbreakable, unstoppable, and forever upheld by Your love.

SPIRITUAL WARFARE PRAYER - BE STRONG & COURAGEOUS

Lord of Heaven's Armies, My Strength and Deliverer,

You have not created me to shrink back. I am called to rise. When fear tries to whisper its lies, let Your voice thunder with greater power. Fill my heart with Holy courage and bold conviction. I refuse to tremble before any giant, for the One who goes before me has already defeated the grave. Strengthen my resolve to obey even when obedience demands sacrifice. Give me the kind of courage that doesn't just fight well, but stands in purity and honor when others cave to compromise.

*Today **I choose faith over fear**, obedience over ease, and courage over comfort.*

Amen.

POWER PRINCIPLE

You are my victory.

SPIRITUAL WARFARE PRAYER – BY THE BLOOD OF THE LAMB

Redeeming Savior, My Deliverer and Defender,

*I overcome, not by human strength, but through the power of the blood of **Jesus Christ** and the testimony You've placed within me. Your sacrifice shattered every accusation and emptied the enemy of his authority. When guilt tries to stalk me, I claim Your blood. When my past rises like a shadow, I declare the victory of the cross. Cleanse me again in Your triumph, Lord. Mark my home, my mind, and my spirit with the crimson seal of redemption. The enemy cannot cross the line of the Lamb's blood You have drawn around me.*

Amen.

POWER PRINCIPLE

Today I stand redeemed, restored, and fully ready for battle.

SPIRITUAL WARFARE PRAYER - LIGHT IN THE DARKNESS

Radiant Savior, Light of the World,

Let Your light blaze through me when shadows try to gather. Darkness has no power over Your radiance, and You have placed that Holy fire within me. When despair tries to close in around my heart, let Your Word break through like dawn and clear my path. I refuse to fear the dark. I am called to invade it. Strengthen me to speak life where there is despair, to carry truth where lies have taken root, and to bring warmth into places grown numb and cold.

Lord, make me a living flame in Your hand, a torch that carries Your presence.

Amen.

POWER PRINCIPLE

Wherever You send me, darkness has no choice but to flee.

DEVOTIONAL 3: COURAGE IN THE BATTLE

✦ **Be Strong and of Good Courage** ✦

Fear often whispers that we are weak, outnumbered, or alone. However, God repeatedly reassures His people: "Be strong and courageous. Do not fear, for I am with you." Courage isn't the absence of fear. It is trusting in God's presence despite your fear.

Joshua faced the Jordan River with all of Israel behind him. The Israelites encountered giants, fortified cities, and many battles. Yet God's command was the same: "Do not be afraid." Why? Because the Lord was with them wherever they went.

As you absorb these vivid images, let these Scriptures serve as reminders that true courage doesn't come from within you but from the God who fights on your behalf. Stand confidently. Hold fast to the Sword of Faith. The Lord remains faithful and will never abandon you in your battles.

🙏 *Prayer: "Lord, give me courage to face what lies ahead. Remind me that You go before me and will never leave me."*

RELECTION QUESTIONS

ourage in the Battle ✦

REFLECT ON THESE QUESTIONS:

1. What challenge or "giant" are you facing right now that calls for bold courage and deeper trust in God's strength rather than your own?
   - How will you use God's armor to defend yourself?
2. Where have you seen God's faithfulness in past battles?
   - How does remembering those victories fuel your confidence in this season?

PART FOUR
ENDURING
TO THE FINISH
(FINAL VICTORY)

ENDURING TO THE FINISH

The walk of faith isn't a quick dash; it's a steady, determined march toward eternal triumph. Every challenge shapes us, every spiritual battle fortifies us, and every step of obedience brings us nearer to the crown waiting for us at the finish. We aren't simply hanging on or barely making it through. We are more than conquerors through Christ, who has claimed us and loves us without measure. The conflict may feel intense, but the victory has already been secured by the blood of the Lamb. So stand firm, hold fast to your faith, and fix your gaze on the One who guides your steps. The finish line is radiant with His glory, and the reward He promises is everlasting.

> *Romans 8:37–39* ~ *"No, in all these things we are more than conquerors through Him who loved us. For I am sure that neither death nor life, nor angels nor rulers, nor things present nor things to come, nor powers, nor height nor depth, nor anything else in all creation, will be able to separate us from the love of God in Christ Jesus our Lord."*

THESE VERSES DELIVER BOLD, unmistakable declarations of God's relentless, unfailing love for His people. They don't simply call us to be brave, but they infuse us with divine strength by proclaiming that we are *"more than conquerors"* through Christ. That word *"more"* changes everything. It doesn't describe someone who barely survives struggle or barely makes it through. It speaks of a believer who rises above what should have crushed them, who walks in victory that goes far beyond mere survival. To be *"more than"* a conqueror means the battle doesn't just end in your favor; it ends in overwhelming triumph because of God's steadfast, undeserved love. In Him, the outcome is not uncertain. The victory is assured.

Paul doesn't stop at declaring our victory in Christ. He goes further by giving us absolute assurance that nothing in existence can sever us from God's love. Angels, demons, hardships, suffering, even death itself ... Paul intentionally covers every realm and every possibility. He leaves no loophole, no corner of creation with the authority to pull a believer away from the love of God. Nothing physical or spiritual, nothing in the past, present, or future has the power to separate us from Him.

These verses also echo a vital truth: God's love is not something we earn. Christ's sacrifice was never deserved; it was freely given. That sacrifice stands as the ultimate proof of God's love and the anchor of our salvation.

In the end, believers are reminded that they can face every trial, storm, and spiritual attack with **unshakable confidence**. God's love rises above every arrow the enemy launches. His love holds us, guards us, and carries us through every battle we will ever face.

2 Timothy 4:7–8 ~ *"I have fought the good fight, I have finished the race, I have kept the faith. Henceforth there is laid up for me the crown of righteousness, which the Lord, the righteous judge, will award to me on that Day."*

IN THESE VERSES, Paul looks back on his life and ministry with the steady confidence of someone who has lived out God's command to be courageous, to endure, and to walk as "more than a conqueror." He pictures himself standing before the Lord, fully assured that he has carried out his calling with faithfulness and resolve.

Paul's use of athletic imagery to describe spiritual endurance has obvious modern applications. It gives us something tangible: the grit, sweat, and determination required to push through pain and pressure. Paul's language paints his journey as one filled with obstacles, yet marked by unwavering commitment because he knows the reward waiting on the other side far outweighs every sacrifice. That prize, the one bestowed by God Himself, is the highest honor any believer could ever hope to receive.

The Greek word Paul uses for "fight" refers to **intense struggle and physical exertion**. It's the kind you'd see in a wrestling match or an MMA bout. Paul is comparing the Christian life to a fierce contest against spiritual forces that press hard and fight dirty. It requires discipline, training, endurance, and the willingness to push past your natural limits with the supernatural strength of God.

Then he shifts to another athletic metaphor: "finished the race." This reveals how Paul viewed the calling of a believer, not as a random journey, but as a path designed by God Himself. The course isn't accidental. It isn't improvised. It is a divine assignment crafted uniquely for each of God's children. At the end of life, each of us will either have run the race laid before us or we will not. Paul declares with conviction that he completed the course God entrusted to him.

And then there's the phrase that threads through Scripture and echoes into our everyday conversations: "kept the faith." Paul held tightly to the truth of Christ. He guarded it. He stood firm in the face of lies and distortions. The same man who once hunted followers of Jesus now speaks as one who spent his life defending the gospel with unwavering loyalty. His story is a testament to transformation, redemption, and steadfast devotion.

And as with any great contest, there is a reward. Just as ancient Greek athletes were crowned with laurel wreaths, Paul speaks of a "Crown of Righteousness," which is a reward given by the Lord to those who have lived faithfully, finished their race, and held fast to the truth. It is a crown not earned by performance, but bestowed by grace upon those who remained obedient and steadfast.

What greater hope could we hold as believers? When our time comes to lay aside this mortal life and cross into eternity, what more could we desire than to be welcomed by our Savior with the reward He has promised: the Crown of Righteousness? To have this crown placed upon the heads of those who fought well, endured faithfully, and kept the faith to the very end is the ultimate win.

Revelation 12:11 ~ *"And they have conquered him by the blood of the Lamb and by the word of their testimony, for they loved not their lives even unto death."*

IN THIS PASSAGE, believers are given yet another powerful insight into God's supernatural protection. The writer reveals that the enemy of every Christian is finally defeated through two unstoppable forces: the blood of Jesus Christ and the bold testimony of God's people. Our faith in Christ's finished work: His sacrifice on the cross, His resurrection, and His ascension is what redeems us, strengthens us, and secures our victory over the grip of sin.

What unnerves Satan most is not human strength, but the believer's unwavering declaration of faith. Your testimony, spoken aloud with conviction, signals his downfall. He knows that praise is the sound of chains breaking. He knows that when a believer loves the truth of Christ more than the comfort of this world, his influence collapses. That is why the enemy trembles; every ounce of his power has already been stripped away by Jesus.

At the center of the Christian life stands the sacrifice of Christ; the cornerstone of everything we believe, everything we hope for, and everything we cling to in battle. Without His freely given, undeserved sacrifice, we would have no defense when spiritual attacks attempt to push us back. But because of Him, we stand.

This verse reminds us that true courage and steadfastness have nothing to do with avoiding hardship or escaping death. Victory in Christ is not defined by self-preservation. Instead, it is found in refusing to let the fear of death dictate our obedience. It is choosing to remain faithful, anchored, and unshaken in the truth of Jesus, no matter the cost.

Stand firm, Warrior. Your victory was sealed long before the battle began.

1 Corinthians 16:13 ~ *"Be watchful, stand firm in the faith, act like men, be strong."*

THIS VERSE MAY USE ONLY a few words, but they carry incredible force. It is a direct call for believers to grow up spiritually, to develop maturity, resolve, and strength as we stand against the evil that surrounds us. And before anyone gets tangled up in modern pronouns, let's clarify: "act like men" is the language of the battlefield. It's not about gender; it's about **steadfastness, discipline**, and **the mindset of a soldier**. This call applies to every follower of Christ, male and female alike.

When Paul says, "be strong," he is speaking of far more than physical strength. He's calling believers into full spiritual adulthood. It's time to step beyond the basics and embrace the responsibility of building, supporting, and defending the body of Christ. We are meant to mature into warriors who not only grow the Church, but guard it against spiritual threats that try to infiltrate and destroy.

This is where self-reflection becomes crucial. Ask yourself:

- Are you putting on God's armor every day?
- Are you walking in courage?
- Are you anchored in His love and confident in His protection?
- Do you remember that salvation is a gift, not something you earn?

These qualities shape a faithful, vigilant, uncompromising Warrior of Christ. Because wearing the Armor of God isn't just about protecting your own heart in a single moment of conflict. It's about standing your ground, defending the Church, strengthening fellow believers, and carrying out the mission Christ modeled during His time on earth.

This is the calling of every spiritual soldier: to protect, to persevere, and to strengthen the body of Christ with unwavering devotion.

Psalm 27:1 ~ *"The Lord is my light and my salvation; whom shall I fear? The Lord is the stronghold of my life; of whom shall I be afraid?"*

AS WE REACH the end of this journey, we circle back to one of the earliest writings in Scripture: a passage from the Book of Psalms. How fitting that a message of strength, hope, and divine protection from King David himself brings this devotional series to a close.

When David calls God his **light**, he isn't describing a soft glow or a pleasant warmth. He's speaking of a blazing torch; a guiding brilliance that cuts through confusion, exposes danger, and provides direction when everything around feels uncertain. Just as we need a light to walk a dark path, God's presence illuminates the way before us. Without His guidance, navigating the traps and deceptions of this world would feel like wandering an endless forest on a moonless night.

David also describes the Lord as his **stronghold**. Not a fragile shelter slapped together with branches, but a fortified refuge; built to withstand attack, endure storms, and protect those inside. A stronghold shields against the elements, against the enemy, and against the relentless pressures of life. It is a place to breathe, to recover, and to meditate on God's Word while waiting for His direction.

And the context makes David's words even more powerful. He wrote this psalm during one of the most distressing periods of his life, when he was a fugitive running from King Saul. Every step came with risk. Every moment carried fear. Yet in the middle of danger and chaos, David anchored himself in God's protection. He trusted that no matter how fierce the threat, no matter how overwhelming the chase, God was greater; stronger than Saul, stronger than the armies pursuing him, and stronger than the fear pounding in his chest.

David understood what we must remember today: **our God is bigger than anything that rises against us, and His faithfulness endures forever.**

SPIRITUAL WARFARE PRAYERS

NOTES

SPIRITUAL WARFARE PRAYER - WHOM SHALL I FEAR

Lord of Light, My Protector and Stronghold,

Your Word proclaims through King David in the Book of Psalms: *"The Lord is my light and my salvation; whom shall I fear?"*

When intimidation tries to creep in, let Your light burst through every shadow. When threats rise around me, remind me that You command Heaven's armies and none can stand against Your power. Fill my heart with boldness born of Your Spirit.

I refuse to fear tomorrow. You already hold it.

I refuse to fear failure. You redeem every broken place.

I refuse to fear death. You have already conquered it forever.

Amen.

POWER PRINCIPLE

I am unafraid. I stand fearless, shielded by Your love and strengthened by Your name.

SPIRITUAL WARFARE PRAYER - OVERCOMER

Risen Savior, My Conqueror and King,

*You have spoken over me that I am an overcomer through the blood of **Jesus Christ** and the authority of Your Word. When I stumble, lift me back to my feet. When doubt tries to shake me, steady my heart. Turn every weakness into a testimony of Your strength, every wound into purpose, and every struggle into Holy resilience. My victory does not come from who I am, but instead, it flows from who You are within me.*

Amen.

POWER PRINCIPLE

The enemy has already been crushed beneath Your feet, and I choose to walk in that triumph today.

SPIRITUAL WARFARE PRAYER – NO WEAPON FORMED AGAINST ME

Lord of Victory, My Fortress and Defender,

*Your Word promises that no weapon formed against me will succeed. Even when the enemy schemes, his plans collapse before they ever reach me. Surround me with Your presence like radiant armor. Let the blood of **Jesus Christ** cover me completely: spirit, mind, and body. I refuse to fear the threats of the enemy, because I am sealed, guarded, and empowered by Your Spirit. Wrap me in Your grace until every attack loses its aim.*

Amen.

POWER PRINCIPLE

Weapons may rise against me, but they will never prevail.

SPIRITUAL WARFARE PRAYER - GOD'S ARMY

Commander of Heaven's Hosts,

You are raising an army; not one fueled by fear, but by faith; not by human strength, but by holy fire. Unite us, Lord, shoulder to shoulder and shield to shield. Let love be the banner we carry and truth the standard we defend. Teach us to wage war with purity, to fight with compassion, and to lead with unwavering courage. And when the battle intensifies, remind us that we never stand alone.

Strengthen Your army, awaken every warrior, and send us forward until every heart has encountered Your glory.

Amen.

POWER PRINCIPLE

I step into my place within Your ranks. I am armed, anointed, and chosen as part of Your victorious army.

SPIRITUAL WARFARE PRAYER - THE BELT OF TRUTH

Lord of Truth, Keeper of Every Promise,

Lord, fasten the belt of Your truth securely around me. In a world drowning in confusion and deceit, make me unshakable in what is eternal. Align my thoughts, my words, and my actions with Your unchanging Word so that no lie can gain a foothold in my life. Expose every falsehood the enemy has ever spoken over me. Silence every voice that twists what You have called good and pure. Wrap me so firmly in Your truth that fear cannot move me, temptation cannot lure me, and pride cannot blind me.

When the enemy whispers doubt, I will answer with Your promises.

When he distorts reality, I will stand upon what You have spoken.

Teach me to walk in honesty, humility, and unwavering conviction. Keep me anchored in the truth that sets me free.

Amen.

POWER PRINCIPLE

Today I gird myself with Your Word, Lord; unshakable, unbreakable, and alive within me.

DEVOTIONAL 4: ENDURING TO THE FINISH

✦ The Crown of Victory ✦

The Christian walk isn't a sprint; it's a long, steady endurance race of faith. Near the end of his life, Paul declared with confidence, "I have fought the good fight, I have finished the race, I have kept the faith." Ahead of him waited the Crown of Righteousness; a reward promised not only to him, but to all who eagerly anticipate Christ's return and faithfully complete the path set before them.

Endurance isn't comfortable. It means holding your ground in seasons of testing, refusing to quit when the road grows steep, and fixing your eyes on Jesus Christ, the One who authors your faith and carries you across the finish line. Yet take comfort in this unbreakable truth: nothing in Heaven or on earth can separate you from the love of God in Christ.

As you move through these pages, picture that end goal, that glorious moment when you will stand before your Savior and hear the words every believer longs for: "Well done, good and faithful servant." Keep pressing forward. Your crown is already waiting in His hands.

🙏 *Prayer: "Lord, help me endure with faith and finish strong. Keep my eyes on the eternal crown that awaits in Your presence."*

REFLECTION QUESTIONS

✦ Enduring to the Finish ✦

REFLECT ON THESE QUESTIONS:

1. **What practices, truths, or reminders help you stay steady and faithful when the path feels long, heavy, or uncertain?**
   - What keeps you moving forward when endurance is the battle?
2. **When you imagine standing before Jesus Christ at the finish line of your race, what words do you most hope to hear from Him?**
   - What affirmation from His heart stirs your soul on the deepest level?

PART FIVE
SPIRITUAL
WARFARE
PRAYER ARMORY

SPIRITUAL WARFARE PRAYERS

✦ **S**piritual Warfare Prayer Armory ✦

WELCOME to the *Spiritual Warfare Prayer Armory*, a sacred vault of battle-tested prayers for every warrior of Christ. You've already encountered many of these prayers throughout your journey in this book, but the pages ahead complete the full Armory Collection. These are not merely sentences on a page; they are spiritual weapons, grounded in Scripture and strengthened through faith. Each prayer has been shaped to awaken boldness, quiet every whisper of fear, and remind you that the Lord of Hosts goes before you, leading the charge in every battle you face.

2 Corinthians 10:4 ~ *"The weapons we fight with are not the weapons of the world. On the contrary, they have divine power to demolish strongholds."*

WHEN YOU PRAY THESE WORDS, you are not releasing empty breath into the atmosphere; you are wielding the Sword of the Spirit, lifting the Shield of Faith, and standing beneath the banner of a victory already secured through Christ. These are not gentle requests; they are declarations of Kingdom authority. Every sentence affirms this truth: you are not weak, helpless, or exposed. You are equipped, empowered, and purposefully positioned for this very moment.

As you move through each page, picture yourself stepping into Heaven's war room. Let your voice rise with conviction, whether it's a quiet whisper in moments of stillness or a fierce cry in the heat of battle. Your prayers do not disappear into the void; they resonate across eternity and reach the very throne of God.

SPIRITUAL WARFARE PRAYERS

NOTES

SPIRITUAL WARFARE PRAYER - UNSHAKEABLE FAITH

God of Endurance and Unshakable Truth,

When storms rise, and the ground beneath me quakes, anchor me in a faith that refuses to falter. Strengthen my spirit when the battle stretches on. Let faith be the solid ground under my feet and the flame that fuels my determination. I will not be swayed by the opinions of others, nor will I tremble at the roar of the enemy. My faith is rooted in Your Word, refined through fire, and proven unbreakable.

Lord, teach me to stand firm until the final moment with my feet planted, heart steady, and eyes locked on You.

Amen.

POWER PRINCIPLE

I fight from the victory already won, not for a victory still uncertain.

SPIRITUAL WARFARE PRAYER - THE SWORD OF THE SPIRIT

Holy Spirit, Breath of God and Living Word,

Place in my hands the sword that never loses its edge: Your living, breathing Word, sharper than any double-edged blade. Teach me to wield it with courage, discernment, and holy confidence. Let Scripture be more than words I speak; let it ignite inside me, cutting through every lie, every fear, and every chain that tries to hold me back. When the enemy whispers defeat, I will respond with Your truth. When temptation calls out to me, I will stand firm upon Your promises. When darkness tries to gather, I will strike with the brilliance of Your Word.

Fill me with boldness to declare what You have spoken:

- *that You alone are Lord,*
- *that victory belongs to **Jesus Christ**,*
- *and that no darkness can extinguish the light of Your truth.*

In the name of Jesus, Amen.

POWER PRINCIPLE

Today I stand as Your warrior, armed with the Sword of the Spirit:
My Weapon of Truth,
My Shield of Hope,
My Banner of Victory.

SPIRITUAL WARFARE PRAYER - FEAR NOT

God of Power and Perfect Love,

You have spoken it to me over and over: Do not fear.

So today, I choose obedience over emotion. When shadows stretch long, and the enemy whispers his threats, let Your steady voice rise above it all: Do not be afraid, for I am with you. Fill my heart with Holy boldness. Drive out every trembling thought with the power of Your love. Remind me that courage isn't the absence of fear; it's choosing to trust You right in the middle of it.

Trade my fear for faith.

Exchange my worry for worship.

Turn my trembling into triumph.

Amen.

POWER PRINCIPLE

In Your strength I fear nothing, for You are everything.

SPIRITUAL WARFARE PRAYER - THE SHIELD OF FAITH

Lord of Hosts, My Protector and Fortress,

Lord, place the mighty shield of faith firmly in my hands. When fear tries to rise, let my shield rise higher. When doubt launches its fiery arrows, let faith extinguish every spark before it comes close to my heart. Strengthen my trust in You when the path grows dim. Teach me to cling to Your promises even when I cannot see the next step. Remind me that faith is not anchored in emotion but in Your unchanging truth.

I refuse to bow to worry. You are my confidence.

I refuse to yield to despair. You are my hope.

Let every breath within me proclaim: My God is faithful. My victory is secure.

Surround me with Your presence so completely that nothing can pierce the peace You provide. Today, I lift my shield high and declare that no weapon formed against me will prevail.

Amen.

POWER PRINCIPLE

I trust in You, Lord: my Defender, my Deliverer, my Faith.

FAITH

SPIRITUAL WARFARE PRAYER - STAND FIRM

Unshakable God, My Rock and Refuge,

*When the winds roar and the ground seems to crumble beneath me, anchor my feet in Your unshakable truth. Teach me to stand firm; not in pride, but in faith; not in fear, but in the strength You provide. Even if the world rages around me, I will not be moved. My confidence is built upon **Jesus Christ**, my Cornerstone and steady foundation.*

Strengthen me to resist every temptation, endure every test, and rise again after every stumble. Keep me from wavering when the enemy shouts or when my flesh feels weary. Lord, I stand armored, steady, and unafraid. The battle belongs to You, and You have never lost.

With Your strength supporting me, I will not retreat.

Amen.

POWER PRINCIPLE

By the power of Your Spirit, I hold the line.

SPIRITUAL WARFARE PRAYER - THE CROWN OF RIGHTEOUSNESS

Faithful Judge and Eternal Rewarder,

You have promised a Crown of Righteousness to all who long for Your appearing. Help me to live each day with that promise fixed before my eyes. Keep my motives pure, my hands clean, and my heart unwavering. I do not fight for applause or human recognition. I contend for Your approval alone. I do not chase after earthly crowns that tarnish and fade, but after the eternal reward You have prepared.

Let righteousness be the garment I wear, the armor that protects me, and the honor that marks my life. Place upon my spirit the unseen Crown of Righteousness that reminds me to whom I belong and what I am running toward.

Amen.

POWER PRINCIPLE

I will run my race with faith, and I will finish it with joy, until the day I lay my crown at your feet.

SPIRITUAL WARFARE PRAYER - MIGHTY WARRIOR

Lord of Glory, My Strength and Champion,

You are the Mighty Warrior who goes before me, clearing the path and leading the charge. Train my hands for battle and shape my heart in obedience to Your voice. When the enemy presses in, remind me that I am never outnumbered. The armies of Heaven stand on my side. Give me the discipline of a seasoned soldier, the humility of a servant, and the unshakable resolve of a conqueror. Make me bold, immovable, and steadfast in every fight.

Amen.

POWER PRINCIPLE

You are my Commander, and every victory belongs to You.

SPIRITUAL WARFARE PRAYER - THE BATTLE BELONGS TO THE LORD

Lord of Hosts, Commander of Heaven's Armies,

I place this battle fully into Your hands. I have carried it too long and fought it in my own strength, but the truth remains: this war does not belong to me; it belongs to You. You go before me in power, surround me with Your presence, and fight for me with unending love. Teach me to trust while You move, to rest while You war on my behalf. Let my praise rise higher than my panic, and let my worship become stronger than my worry.

I step back so You can step forward, for the fight is Yours alone.

Amen.

POWER PRINCIPLE

Victory is sure through Jesus Christ.

SPIRITUAL WARFARE PRAYER - NEVER SURRENDER

Lord of Power and Everlasting Glory,

I will not retreat. Even when the battle stretches long and the fire burns fierce, I will stand firm in the strength of my God. When my own strength reaches its end, be the endurance that carries me. When hope flickers, ignite it again like flame in my spirit. Let perseverance rise as my praise and worship become my weapon. I may bend beneath the storm's weight, but I will not break, for Your Spirit sustains and strengthens me.

The cross is my banner, the blood my seal, and the crown of life my promised reward. Lord, I will never surrender, because You never did.

Amen.

POWER PRINCIPLE

I refuse to surrender, and I march forward in Your name.

CLOSING BLESSING

A Prayer and Claim of Strength and Victory

HEAVENLY FATHER,

Thank You for the armor You have provided me.

Wrap me in Your truth.

Cover me with Your righteousness.

Steady and direct my steps in the gospel of peace.

Shield me with unwavering faith.

Guard my mind with certain salvation.

And arm me with the sword of Your Spirit.

Let me stand fearless in the battles of life, knowing no weapon formed against me shall prosper.

Hold me steadfast until the day I finish the race and receive the Crown of Righteousness in victory.

Ephesians 6:10 ~ *"Finally, my brethren, be strong in the Lord, and in the power of his might."*

PAY IT FORWARD

A SMALL FAVOR, PLEASE ...

Now that you're fully equipped to Put On the Full Armor of God, you have the opportunity to pass that strength forward. Your voice can help other readers discover the same encouragement, clarity, and spiritual confidence you've gained. By sharing your honest thoughts on Amazon, TikTok, or any store where this book is available, you guide fellow believers toward the help they're searching for.

Your review truly matters.

When you're ready, visit the Book Description page to leave your feedback on Amazon, or the marketplace where you found this book.

Thank you for taking the time to support this message and may God bless you abundantly for it.

BIBLIOGRAPHY

✦ BIBLIOGRAPHY ✦

The Holy Bible, New International Version (NIV)

Biblica, Inc. (2011). *The Holy Bible, New International Version.* Colorado Springs, CO: Biblica, Inc. Used by permission. All rights reserved worldwide.

The Holy Bible, King James Version (KJV)

Cambridge University Press (1769; originally published 1611). *The Holy Bible, King James Version.* Public Domain.

Strong's Exhaustive Concordance of the Bible

Strong, James. *Strong's Exhaustive Concordance of the Bible.* Nashville, TN: Abingdon Press, 1890.

Easton's Bible Dictionary

Easton, M. G. *Easton's Bible Dictionary.* New York: Thomas Nelson & Sons, 1897.

Matthew Henry's Commentary on the Whole Bible

Henry, Matthew. *Matthew Henry's Commentary on the Whole Bible.* Peabody, MA: Hendrickson Publishers, 1991 (Original work published 1706).

Vine's Expository Dictionary of Biblical Words

Vine, W. E. *Vine's Expository Dictionary of Biblical Words.* Nashville, TN: Thomas Nelson, 1940.